Welcome to Iran

By Elma Schemenauer

The
Child's World

Published by The Child's World®
1980 Lookout Drive
Mankato, MN 56003-1705
800-599-READ
www.childsworld.com

Content Adviser: Professor Paul Sprachman, Vice Director,
Center for Middle Eastern Studies, Rutgers, The State University
of New Jersey, New Brunswick, NJ
Design and Production: The Creative Spark, San Juan, Capistrano, CA
Editorial: Publisher's Diner, Wendy Mead, Greenwich, CT
Photo Research: Deborah Goodsite, Califon, NJ

Cover and title page photo: Jon Arnold Images/SuperStock
Interior photos: Alamy: 8 (Wilmar Photography); AP Photo: 12, 13 left (Sayaad), 17, 23, 27
(Vahid Salemi), 19, 21 top, 24 (Hasan Sarbakhshian); Corbis: 18, 22 (Earl & Nazima Kowall);
Getty Images: 7 bottom (Keyvan Behpour/Photonica), 3, 14 (Bruno Morandi/Reportage), 25
(Sebastian D'Souza/AFP), 26 (Behrouz Mehri/AFP), 30 (Reza Estakhrian/Reportage);
iStockphoto.com: 11 (Graeme Gilmour), 28 (Paul Cowan), 29 (Olga Lyubkina), 31 (Klaas
Lingbeek-van Kranen); Landov: 13 right, 20 (Caren Firouz/Reuters); Lonely Planet Images:
3 bottom, 7 top, 10, 16 (Chris Mellor); NASA Earth Observatory: 4 (Reto Stockli); Photolibrary
Group: 3 middle, 9, 15, 21 bottom; Susan Sprachman: 6.
Map: XNR Productions: 5

Library of Congress Cataloging-in-Publication Data
Schemenauer, Elma.
  Welcome to Iran / by Elma Schemenauer.
    p. cm. — (Welcome to the world)
  Includes index.
  ISBN 978-1-59296-972-2 (library bound : alk. paper)
  1. Iran—Juvenile literature. I. Title. II. Series.

DS254.75.S342 2008
955—dc22
                                       2007034773

Contents

Where Is Iran?

What if you were on a flying carpet soaring high above Earth? You would see huge land areas with water around them. These land areas are called **continents.** Some continents are made up of several countries. Iran is in the southwestern part of the continent of Asia.

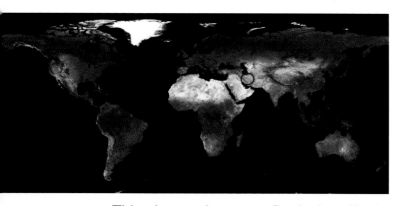

This picture gives us a flat look at Earth. Iran is inside the red circle.

Iran borders the Gulf of Oman to the south and the Persian Gulf to the southwest. West of Iran is Iraq. North of Iran are the Caspian Sea and several countries, including Armenia and Turkmenistan. East of Iran are the countries of Afghanistan and Pakistan.

Did you know?

Iran is really called "The Islamic Republic of Iran." People often just say "Iran" for short. It used to be called Persia.

4

The Land

In the north, along the Caspian Sea, is a moist, green lowland that has Iran's richest soils. Many of its people live there. In the south and southwest, along the Gulf of

A rice field near the Caspian Sea

Oman and Persian Gulf, is another lowland. Its southwestern end has some of Iran's richest oil fields.

In the north and west there are mountains. In Iran's middle and eastern parts is a high plain. Two deserts make up most of this plain. They are covered mostly by sand and gravel or by a crunchy crust of salt.

The Alborz Mountains (above) and the ruins of a desert fort (below)

Dates, a type of fruit, grow on some palm trees.

Plants and Animals

Many of Iran's plants grow in the northern lowland and the mountains. Trees include elms, oaks, cypresses, and walnut trees. In the southern and southwestern lowland, date palms and other trees grow where they get enough water.

In the deserts, thorny shrubs struggle to live. Here and there across Iran are **oases.** Oases are areas watered by underground springs. In Iran's oases, grape vines and mulberry, willow, and poplar trees grow.

Iran's animals include bears, wild sheep and goats, gazelles, and foxes. Birds include storks, falcons, pheasants, and partridges. Lizards skittle across the dry deserts.

A stork near Shiraz

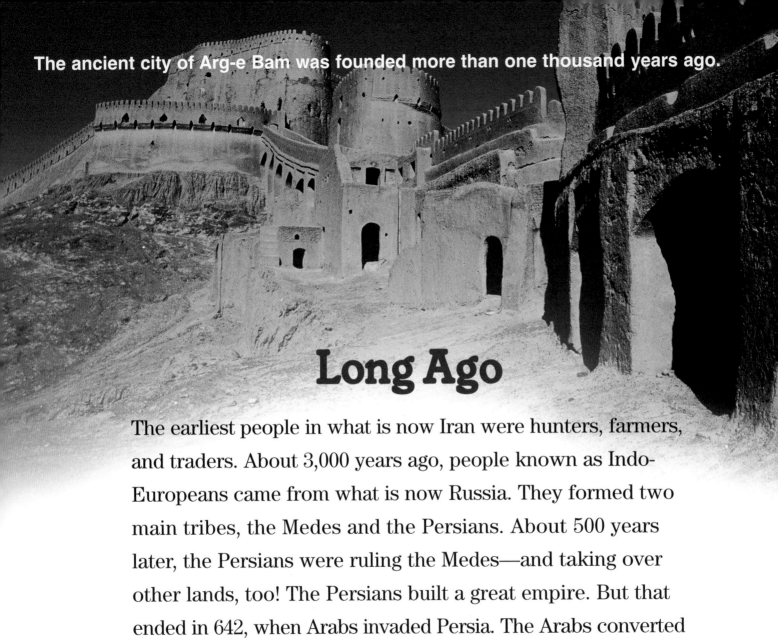

The ancient city of Arg-e Bam was founded more than one thousand years ago.

Long Ago

The earliest people in what is now Iran were hunters, farmers, and traders. About 3,000 years ago, people known as Indo-Europeans came from what is now Russia. They formed two main tribes, the Medes and the Persians. About 500 years later, the Persians were ruling the Medes—and taking over other lands, too! The Persians built a great empire. But that ended in 642, when Arabs invaded Persia. The Arabs converted

10

many of the people to the religion of **Islam.** More invaders came and went, but the country stayed Islamic.

In the early 1900s, oil was found in the area. Starting in 1925, Reza **Shah** Pahlavi, the king, used money from oil to build highways, factories, and seaports. He brought in Western (European and American) ideas and ways of life. In 1935 he changed Persia's name to Iran, which means "land of the Aryans." The Aryans were an ancient people who lived in Iran and the surrounding area.

Did you **know?**

Iran is one of the world's oldest countries. The Bible mentions some of its leaders, such as Cyrus, who was the king of Persia.

11

Iran Today

Mohammad (with crown), the shah of Iran, and his family

In 1941 Reza Shah's son, Mohammad, became the king, or shah. Like his father, he brought many changes to Iran. But many Iranians didn't like him, so in 1979 he was forced leave. Islamic religious leader Ayatollah Khomeini took over, and the Islamic Revolution began. Western ideas and clothes were thrown out. Women had to wear head coverings and dresses down to their toes. Everyone was supposed to obey the laws of a strict

Ayatollah Khomeini (left) led the Islamic Revolution. Today, Mahmoud Ahmadinejad (right) serves as Iran's president.

kind of Islam. In 1989, Ayatollah Khomeini died. Under the new ayatollah, Ali Khamenei, very little changed.

Khamenei remains the country's supreme leader today. He also works with the president to govern the nation. In 2005, Mahmoud Ahmadinejad became Iran's president. The new president is not friendly with the West. He has spoken out against the United States and other western countries.

Three nomad children pose for a photograph.

The People

A nomad family is on the move.

The largest number of Iranians are Indo-Europeans like those who arrived long ago. Most of the Indo-Europeans are Persians, who often live in cities or settled farming areas. Among Iran's other Indo-Europeans are Kurds, Lurs, and Bakhtiaris. Some of these people are **nomads,** moving from place to place to find food and water for their animals.

Many Iranians are related to the people of Turkey. They include Turkomans and Azerbaijanis. Iran also has small numbers of other people, including Arabs, Assyrians, and Armenians.

15

A busy city, Tabriz was founded in ancient times.

City Life and Country Life

Two children study in their living room in Tehran.

In cities, many Iranians live in brick or cement houses or apartments. Since many areas seldom get rain, roofs are often flat. People use them as breezy places to talk, play games, and relax. Inside, Iranians often sit not on chairs but on cozy carpets patterned in red, gold, black, and other colors. Families may serve their meals on carpets as well.

In country villages where people live all year, many houses are much like those in cities. A number of country people, however, are nomads. Since they move around to find grassland for their sheep, goats, and other animals, many live in tents made of felt or other materials.

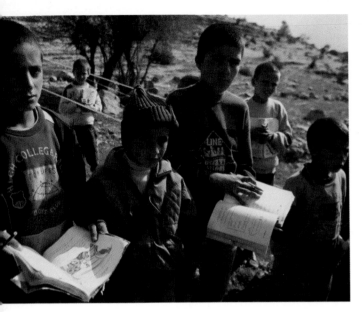

These children attend a traveling school.

Schools and Language

Many Iranian children start school at age six. Most schools stay in one place, but schools for nomads move right along with the nomads. Boys and girls attend separate classes. The most important thing they study is their religion, Islam. Its holy book, the **Koran,** is written in Arabic.

Iran's official language, however, is Farsi, or Persian. It is related to the languages of India and Europe, including English. Farsi uses the Arabic alphabet plus four extra letters. Farsi, unlike English, is written from right to left.

18

A group of girls listen to their teacher on the first day of school.

A woman works on a rug at a factory in Mashad.

Work

Many Iranians pump oil out of the ground, **refine** it, and use it to make goods such as plastics, detergents, and jet fuel. Others work with natural gas. Some mine iron or copper, or collect desert salt to sell. Some work in factories making TV sets, washing machines, engines, shoes, and cloth. Iranian hand weavers make Persian carpets, which are famous around the world.

Farmers grow pistachios, almonds, wheat, rice, tea, fruit, and sugar beets. Among the animals raised are sheep, goats, cattle, water buffalo, chickens, and camels. Some Iranians fish for salmon and sturgeon.

Iran continues to produce a lot of oil today.

Fishermen return home after a long day at sea.

21

Food

Rice, grown in the moist Caspian Sea lowland, is one of Iran's most important foods. People eat it with chicken, fish, beef, carrots, lentils, or beans. For breakfast people often eat bread with cheese, honey, or **halvah,** which is a sweet paste.

Iranians enjoy yogurt. They eat it by itself or in a soup with barley and onions. They also use yogurt to flavor lamb for a popular dish, lamb kebabs with rice. Some of the fruits Iranians grow and eat are dates, oranges, grapes, apples, and Persian melons. Tea is their favorite drink. It is against the Islamic religion to drink wine or other alcoholic drinks, or to eat pork.

A family gathers together for lunch.

People shop for nuts and other treats at a store in Tehran.

Iranians invented polo, a sport played on horseback.

Pastimes

Skiing in the mountains, swimming, soccer, **polo,** horse racing, weight lifting, and wrestling are favorite sports in Iran. Another sport is a mix of wrestling and gymnastics. Found almost nowhere else in the world, it takes place in Iranian clubs called *zurkhanehs*.

Chess is a popular game in Iran.

Among games Iranians enjoy are backgammon and chess. They also watch TV and films. Iranian filmmakers are known for making good films. But they must be careful, since everything shown on screen in Iran is supposed to follow strict Islamic rules.

Holidays

For many Iranians, an important yearly holiday is No Ruz, or New Year's. Other holidays are the prophet Muhammad's birthday and **Ramadan,** a month of daytime fasting. On February 11 Iranians celebrate the Magnificent Victory of the Islamic Revolution of Iran. On that day they remember Ayatollah Khomeini's takeover of the government in 1979.

Outsiders often have a hard time understanding Iran. Today the country faces new challenges. Some Iranian leaders want to stay with Khamenei's strict governing

Families sometimes celebrate No Ruz by having picnics.

Men march in a parade holding Islamic flags.

style. Others want more freedom for women and for people with different political ideas. It will be interesting to see what happens.

Area: About 636,000 square miles (1.6 million square kilometers)—a bit bigger than Alaska

Population: More than 68 million people

Capital City: Tehran

Other Important Cities: Mashhad, Isfahan, Tabriz, and Shiraz

Money: The rial

National Language: Persian

National Flag: The flag has three sideways stripes of green, white, and red. On the inside edges of the green and red stripes are the words "Allah Akbar" (God is Great). In red, in the middle of the white stripe, is Iran's coat of arms.

Head of Government: The Grand Ayatollah of Iran (national religious leader) and the president of Iran.

Famous People:

Shirin Ebadi: winner of a Nobel Peace Prize for her work with women and children

Ferdowsi: ancient Persian poet

Ehsan Haddadi: famous athlete, discus thrower

Hafez: Persian poet in the 1300s

Mohammad Khatami: former president

Abbas Kiarostami: film director

Hashemi Rafsanjani: former president

National Song: The National Anthem of the Islamic Republic of Iran

> Upwards on the horizon rises the Eastern Sun,
> The sight of the true religion.
> Bahman—the brilliance of our faith.

> Your message, O Imam, of independence and freedom is imprinted on our souls.

> O Martyrs! The time of your cries of pain rings in our ears.
> Enduring, continuing, eternal,
> The Islamic Republic of Iran.

Iranian Recipe: Saffron-flavored ice cream

Saffron is a popular spice in Iran. It has a mild, sweet taste and adds a golden color to foods. First, take the ice cream out of the freezer and let thaw for 5 to 10 minutes. Then put 1 teaspoon of saffron into 1 tablespoon of hot water in a small bowl. Let this rest for a few minutes.

Once the ice cream has softened, put it in a large bowl and add the saffron mixture. Stir well. Add pistachios on top and put the ice cream in the freezer. After a few hours, your sweet treat will be ready to eat!

How Do You Say...

ENGLISH	FARSI	HOW TO SAY IT
hello	salam	sah-LAHM
good-bye	khoda hafez	koh-DAH ha-FEZ
please	lotfan	lot-FAN
thank you	mamnoonam	mam-NOON-am
one	yek	YEK
two	do	DOH
three	seh	SEH
Iran	Iran	ee-RRAN

30

Glossary

continents (KON-tih-nents) Most of Earth's land areas are in huge sections called continents. Iran is located on the continent of Asia.

halvah (HAL-vuh) Halvah is a sweet paste. Many Iranians eat bread with halva for breakfast.

Islam (IS-lahm) Islam is a set of beliefs about God (called Allah) and his prophet Muhammad. Many people in Saudi Arabia belong to the Islamic faith.

Koran (koh-RRAHN) The Quran is the holy book of the religion of Islam. Many Iranians follow the Islamic faith.

nomads (NOH-madz) Nomads are people who move from place to place rather than living in one home. Some Iranians are nomads.

oases (oh-AY-seez) Oases are places in the desert that get water from underground springs. Most oases have green plants and trees.

polo (POH-loh) Polo is a game where players ride on horses and try to hit a ball with a mallet. Polo is a popular sport in Iran.

Ramadan (RAH-muh-dahn) Ramadan is an Islamic religious holiday. During Ramadan, people do not eat between sunrise and sunset.

refine (ree-FINE) When you refine something, you get rid of the parts you don't want. Many Iranians refine oil to make fuels and other products.

shah (SHAH) Iran's king was called a shah. In 1979, the Shah of Iran was replaced by Ayatollah Khomeini.

Further Information

Read It

Doak, Robin S. *Iran*. Minneapolis, MN: Compass Point Books, 2004.

Kaplan, Leslie C. *A Primary Source Guide to Iran*. New York: PowerKids Press, 2005.

Richardson, Adele. *Iran*. Mankato, MN: Creative Education, 2007.

Sheen, Barbara. *Foods of Iran*. San Diego, CA: KidHaven Press, 2006.

Look It Up

Visit our Web page for lots of links about Iran:
http://www.childsworld.com/links

Note to Parents, Teachers, and Librarians: We routinely verify our Web links to make sure they are safe, active sites—so encourage your readers to check them out!

Index